THE
VIEW FROM
THE PEACOCK'S
TAIL

THE VIEW FROM THE PEACOCK'S TAIL

POEMS BY

M. L. ROSENTHAL

New York   OXFORD UNIVERSITY PRESS   1972

Certain of these poems appeared first
in *Antaeus, The Humanist, The Nation,
The New York Quarterly, The New York Times,
Phantomas* (**Brussels**), *The Quarterly Review
of Literature, Salmagundi,* and *Shenandoah.*

for Victoria

CONTENTS

1

*HIS
PRESENT
DISCONTENTS* a sequence

for Ramon Guthrie
"the winning and the losing cost the same"

I TO HIS OTHER SPIRIT
"There comes over me some days a feeling, abundant, political . . ." (Vallejo)

I know you so well, not at all, beloved
apple of my bough, heart's-thorn, wise little spirit
who will outlive me, and my fear for you, and yours
for me in the world's wide room where through all my weathers
I move, walk, ride, dream in my pants like Einstein's or
Lenin's, full of the latest wrinkles at seat or knee,
posh as somebody's grandpa darkening on an old daguerreotype.

"We are transmitters," Lawrence said, but you will rise
on an arc of your own nature, beautiful, beyond even yourself—
who knows what it will be like then? Does not every life,
every painting, poem dance out the grief of beauty and joy?
"There comes over me some days a feeling, abundant, political," when
      I think of you
(floating forever, as you know, in my own amniotic soul
where something of you took form, mother to myself as well) . . .
stormy, volatile, tentative as all living thought. But you have been born
and will be again, airy creature— myself, and far from me.

On a bed, shooting up with your hepatitopoeic needles,
"fuck" and "shit" on the tip of your tongue's pride, music
   of wrathful vileness, time dripping away
   from the crusted corners of your seraph's-eyes while
   the retch-stale air of your closed-chamber dreams
   sucks in the drowsy host of sullen flies, friends
   settling in, companionable death-row prison-mates,
   and the invisible sun and stars and moon
   swing overhead singing death's immortal sway—

and the earth, they say, swings 'round the sun,
   the days become the seasons, the seasons the years,
   and we in our ignorance swaying our plumed and cocked bodies
   while time grows crystal in the soul. You have arisen
   from your grimy couch, opened your brilliant eyes, put sighing
   aside the womb-bliss of needles, and wavered forth.
   Dawn waits, still unseen, but the richest suns, sometimes,
   spill through the sullied winter-sky. And the clear
   dance of thought, grateful as a flogged puppy, resumes
   and the charmed charnel fountain-play of poems, midwinter spring indeed!

Oh, I could speak Chinese, perceive how doorbells work,
lead bloodless revolutions skipping through the parks, roll
the whole dismantled creation into one gentle poem, bouncing like a ball
for children to throw and old men glaze with their grateful tears.
The skulls of Kiev, Oswiecim, Songmy, Gettysburg
will thunder underground toward the tenpins of Jerusalem
and on the Day of Judgment rocket upwards chanting
of the miracle that was life, that dreamed to walk on water,
that swallowed all that was, and then was not.

II   JAMMED UP

I write in this fragrant garden not a hundred yards from where Keats once lived. He was like me in this, that he was a temporary sojourner amid all these fragrances and colors, this stillness poised between the sounds of the great city and the coot-haunted heath close by.

It is a time of removal for me, not complete but true removal. I am still in the midst of "everything." Common mortality has touched me. Mother, father, stepfather, half-brother, dead. How am I to reach back into all their lives? Into that precarious, passionate reality? Do I want to? Do I believe in that reality? Choice and necessity are merely, are they not, the hardening of the arbitrary? But that "arbitrary"— it's not personal whim, not "conditions," but something too often deadly and squalid: human reality.

I have a "tragic view of life" *and* an optimistic "nature." What has that to do with anything? I know that others, many others, have a more sharply defined sense of themselves. They have plans that are meant, first to increase our unease, but then to destroy it. They mean to be alive, at the heart of power, of the senses, to touch the very shock of reality. But are they closer to it than I? I should like to look into this inquiry, which has been going on all my life. At the point of conviction I stand amazed, my eyes turned into oceans where "lost swimmers" churn.

All these ironies, these quotation-marks. *I* say, let us be committed to whom and what we desire. Let us act as men must. But what, why, do I mean?

III AM I THAT DANCER?

This very dusk, intangible velvet,
my fingers are walking through you, my eyes listen,
you have taken me at one touch, I dance on your rooftops—

Am I that dancer now, whom once I saw
top-hatted, gloved, in evening pumps,
footing it swiftly, an inch above Fifth Avenue,
dream-dandy flitting toward unimaginable gaiety
like the thought of joy skimming among gravestones?

His shoes had tiny wings of light.
He paused at the corner for the traffic to pass,
then sparkled across the street and was gone.

IV NOT QUITE WHAT I MEANT

As I must start *somewhere* (not counting false starts, or should we?), I shall plunge into the first ocean that occurs to me: Revolution. I realize that you cannot call a somewhere an ocean without meaning that it's too deep to fathom at once.— At any rate, Revolution.

At once I must face some realities I can't quite think what to do about. I am for Revolution, though I believe that, at the same time, I am impossibly apart. It is impossibly apart to hate rudeness, violence, grossness, overstatement. And these seem inseparable from Revolution. You will say, "Thank God the question is in the hands of others who always seem to know what to do, those leaders of men who have already taken us to the heights we now command. They have taught us to fight, to win, to die like heroes, to kill ourselves rather than be humiliated, to accept defeat and wait for another day, to see life strategically, to master tactics, to know how to rule and be ruled, to know how to organize armies, how to move in the dark, how to strike the enemy suddenly without hindrance from women and children (or how to sacrifice women and children while choking back our tears), how to see to it that bridges are built and projectiles flown to other planets."

It's not quite what I meant. It was simpler than all that.

Is the situation desperate?

Is will but the subjective dimension of fate?

Who decides that *this* is the moment when humanity must be dismantled?

V WORKING

Working slowly, your way, through the air
working slowly, into your own brain's maze
if that's the way it works
till you've worked it through

Still, still, it won't work
You'll never work it out
You'll never work around it

It's, just, dead, center.

Work it up and out, the dead stump?
It, just, happens, to
be you.

VI   HOW DID IT HAPPEN?

On the subject of Revolution again: The basic position is unassailable. Why? Because an infinite series of improvements is clearly possible in any institution, and because all process is far more open and fluid than anyone can possibly understand in any given moment, and because institutions themselves are not ordained by God.

All institutions have evolved as the formalizations of innumerable improvised expedients. There is no reason to believe that any one of them is the best of all possible institutions.

"We are at liberty, not only to propose every kind of change, but to do away with our institutions entirely if that is our will." (Document signed by Adam, Eve, Snake, Cain, Abel. God abstaining.) As Yeats has it,

Many ingenious lovely things are gone
That seemed sheer miracle to the multitude. . . .

Yeats spoke of cycles of history, the rise into ascendancy of different modes of thought and personality in different eras. But he was too bound by the sense of *some* meaningful order, however incommensurate with man's needs, to see the true arbitrariness of our choices. The pity of our loss, yes— those dearly bought "many ingenious lovely things" that are gone forever. But the full horror of statistical man was hidden from him, statistical man with his "random" behavior. When man invented that statistical image of himself, when he decided that we are as reducible as other objects, he was ruling himself banished from the realm of pure making. The barbarism of the past was that of gross, unevolved man. The barbarism of the present is that of evolved man, who has not yet seized the creative moment when he might have brought awe and kindness into harmony with one another.

With awe and kindness in harmony, keeping intact man's vision of himself, what changes might we not be able to contemplate? Without them, man must hammer his image down again to flat, elementary metal, faceless and without memory.

How did it happen that, just when we thought to enter the new kingdom of man, our dearest loves, the young, would have no more of that dream?

Ah, that is history! We are not what we thought we were!

VII THE TRUTH

It is not true that "our dearest loves, the young, would have no more of that dream."

The present discontents show that reality has broken into the dream, for the better and for the worse. Reality! Fulfillment at once! Not to delay an instant longer!

All power to us! Power is as power does!

The weak, the tentative, the gentle, those who fear reality must go the wall.

An arrogant simplicity fills the air.

So do the sighs and stench from battlefield and prison, from hospital, slum, and asylum.

VIII VIOLENCE

Poets of Bengal, the wash of the great sea-stench
must, at last, seal even your tongues and ears.
The clamorous life-stench, we see now, was but
the overture breathed by man's genius to the end of this silence.

The killer has balls and a belly, like mine.
The soles of his feet sweat, like mine.
I'm in a hardening world inside, like his.
The world's full of my kills. I've every
weaker man in my helpless grasp, like him.

I can't sort myself out from this great tidal wave,
millions drowning under millions, till all men are silent at last.

Like a wave breaking around, but not over, beauty's solitude,
my own surging halts at the tide-line, then hurries back over
        hissing sands,
and I learn it was not fear of violence but my own sure forgetting—
it was not conquest my own solitude sought, but to break in waves
        about beauty—
that made the wave of my yearning to leap like a squadron of lancers,
        then silently drop
away again, from that marble image on the hissing sands.

IX CRUELTY

As I walk down a city street, a knot of children are playing about the front stairway of an old wooden house. Suddenly a girl of ten, lean, bitter, kicks the shin of a five-year-old boy with all her might. He falls whimpering to the sidewalk. I stop to remonstrate with the girl or comfort the boy— it is confusing— and adult faces, cursing me, explode at the window.

I remember another time. My wife had taken our baby son to a city playground. A little girl there (she might have been the same one) walked up to him and slapped his face sharply. Absolutely impersonal.

And further back, when my younger brother and I were both small children. One day he came home screaming. Some boys had tied a cord around his genitals, a fact we did not discover at once.

Sometimes, when I am dismayed by the rudeness or the violence of the young, I recall the suave, smiling cruelties of those in power, how they use their own authority, and "the rules," and even their knowledge and wisdom, to break the hopes of others. Then the rudeness or violence of the young seems touching!— an inarticulate response forced on them to their disadvantage, including that great disadvantage of feeling in the wrong. But I must remember, too, that cruelty of every sort has its own laws, not to be explained away.

X SCORPIONS

My beautiful young friends are aging gracefully now.
Soon they will be twinkling old gentlemen and ladies.
We never shout at each other now when we meet.
We are always delighted with each other now when we meet.

Once we prowled like panthers, or skunks, in each other's lairs.
We laughed too much, or we bristled, under each other's magic.
Sexual heat, tropic steam, misted our vision.
Impaled on our own nobility, we thought our passions depraved.

Sedately at family dinner, we devoured our prettier cousins,
raping them and our younger aunts at half-past the soup.
Hard, proud as our bodies, we accepted the bounty
of our elders (their lives) indifferently, after a quarrel.

Some of us actually died, or were actually killed; some actually did kill.
Blood leaked terror over us, staining our monstrous regiment.
What were we? What are we? Sentimental scorpions?
Yes, just like old Yahweh, in whose image we were cast.

XI "TO BODIES GONE": PYGMALION REMEMBERING
"See, how everything opens out; thus do we . . ." (Rilke)

Worlds of ivory nakedness . . . faces smiling and Chinese under tossing hair, the painted marble eyes fixed on some distant inward prospect. Incredible frail, silken shoulders, narrow, blushing breasts, and that ludicrously simple, cartoonist's slash that conceals world within world within world, itself only just not concealed by the frond of sweet maidenhair . . . the face and body of anonymous, amazing womanliness, insistent on itself, its uniqueness, its name and station as are the waves that come storming towards the shore to shock and engulf us forever, here, now, where everything flowers in one moment.

Rising and falling astride me, terribly intent. The eyes now bright, with pupils dilated, and now tightly clenched. That pale, self-enclosed face going completely inward. The delicate stalk of body swaying and rocking over the slender, mobile, yet still marble thighs. The breasts still marble, rigid, yet swaying, the painted nipples actually hot! Pausing for one endless moment, eyes staring, seeing and unseeing, here and gone on the hissing Cyprian sands.

XII

BALANCING

on   both   hands

emptiness

DOWN
comes
the
one
handful

DOWN
comes
the
other

the whole

weight   of   space!

2

NOTATIONS
OF
LOVE

SCHLAFLIED

Einmal, wenn ich dich verlier,
wirst du schlafen können, ohne
dass ich wie eine Lindenkrone
mich verflüstre über dir?

Ohne dass ich hier wache und
Worte, beinah wie Augenlider,
auf deine Brüste, auf deine Glieder
niederlege, auf deinen Mund?

Ohne dass ich dich verschliess
und dich allein mit Deinem lasse,
wie einen Garten mit einer Masse
von Melissen und Sternanis?

— Rainer Maria Rilke

LULLABY
(after Rilke's "Schlaflied")

Some day, when I lose you,
will you be able to sleep then,
without my whispering, like a crown of linden
rustling into silence, above you?

Without my watching here, without
my words, soft as eyelids almost,
brushing down on your breasts, on your limbs
gently, and on your lips?

Without my leaving you, eased,
folded shut within yourself at last
like a garden, a mass
of melissas and star-anise?

VARIATION ON A THEME BY RILKE
("Einmal, wenn ich dich verlier . . .")

Some day, when I lose you,
I'll think how lightly
the days came and went while
I was finding you.

The days opened on you:
the light touched you so gently—
secret aureole
cradling your moments.

LATE AT NIGHT

Peering out into the dark
gets you your face thrown right back at you
through the window-pane.

Everything flings back
out of the dark into the light of yourself—
ennui of unprejudiced thought.

Do you know the little zoo
in Golders Hill Park—
the peacocks there?

Feathered Orients,
sheen of metallic blaze and blue
and those all but invisible heads, almost intaglio,

one-dimensional,
murderous, perhaps, if they struck,
pressed into their glittering, turning shields.

Lo, how he turns,
hoping for the peahen's best
(if he notices when it happens),

endlessly patient – and suddenly
the Maharajah of Dacca
has his back to me!

I'm backstage!
O unrehearsed rear of the Real,
the view from the peacock's tail!

Everything gone brown-grey, barnyard-homey,
and all that proud shield of glory up front
flung into his audience from what's back here.

Yes, Achilles behind *his* shield, just stricken,
must have seen himself all the way back here
where everything *really* happens.

Here's where the claws touch earth.
Here's whence the peahen's trodden.
Here the dropping, all that's vulnerable, all the damned tautology –

Great, outspread, oppressive wings of the commonplace,
towering above, behind us,
shriek of the chaotic, denying glory!

I turned my burning shield toward you,
and you, yours, to me.
Did we see, through the reflections, some glimmer

of one real another, standing
back here, back there, peering
into the darkness between?

To think that I wanted
to pierce back through your eyes
into the brain, the being, the worlds around "you"!

Can I touch the world without treading it?
Know the suffering without redoubling it?
Love without hunching the whole of my peacock's back along?

EACH DAY BEATS DOWN

Each day beats down upon
this staunchest flower
in any garden, that ever
in any weather
bloomed at the whirlwind's center.

A sudden joy. Golden
petals open. This one
dizzy bee finds this storied
uncompromising glory.

TO WILFRED OWEN, 1893-1918
"Weep, you may weep, for you may touch them not."

Owen, though I'm no girl
I weep for what I cannot touch:
the irrevocable, dismembered, unknown loves,
sweet holding of all that might ever have been.

As I could not, you saw:
our living sex betrays the grotesque dead.
Traitorous, older, later,
I hold fast my sweetest knowledge.

"Red lips are not so red
   as the stained stones kissed by the English dead"—
I can't think past your young outcry
   nor despise my traitorous knowledge.

NOTATIONS OF LOVE

I YOUR PASSION PLEASES ME

It pleases me. There's
a white dusty car, a white cloud, a mid-March wind
all rushing past. Swallows, flying leaves, shadows left
from the dead winter's last late afternoon. Wild ducks
are flying by. I want
to meet you suddenly on the street
coming to me out of the brightest, blue-
est sky, almost terrible.

Come flying on this wind!

II INCREDULOUS, OUR BODIES ARE REMEMBERING

Incredulous, our bodies are remembering.
Our loins are heavy, remembering
the sweet penetration, holding it.
It holds, strange distant perfume
in the cold and champagne air:
ourselves, we, essence of us
far away and present to our inner touch.

III   IN THE BURNING GLASS—

at the pinpoint of flame, where flesh
concenters all unceasing, hurling, driven spirit
in the marriage bed of our love, there bursts
before our dismayed ecstasy
the terrible human face of need—

the dead face longing to return,
face of the swollen-bellied babe with heavy-drooping eyelids.

IV   ODE ON A YOUNG WOMAN'S CONFESSION

Happens all the time, whether I know you or not.

I see you there, all night on the narrow bed,
walls of your lust pressing in on you, "not letting it happen"
though you're clipped in his arms. "Terrible to desire someone
you detest." Male arrogance thrusting itself on you
and you want but won't let it. . . . You

"rather enjoyed it." The sherry bottle (ugh) was
almost emptied. How many hours thus, "with my clothes on,"
toying with the two vanities, not letting the other's "win," not
letting it "lose," the heavy cudgel fencing
with your whole body while the boat rocked. You "felt sick"
next morning. It held, still holds, your imagination,
like an aborted soul, immortal though unborn. Unpossessed, you
were opened into nonetheless. "His arrogance disgusted me"
nevertheless.

       Dizzy
as though I myself were there in the rocking boat now. The
woman-confusion of the thing, that a man hardly understands,
comes over me too sharply. You were "glad it had happened"!
While I, irrelevantly, am turned away from life
just this moment, just to catch it all for this instant so sharply.

V FIRST MORNING OF JANUARY

First morning of January: brilliant cold smile of this new year.
My love and I awoke together, warm and smiling.
A mid-March wind had carried the months away.
Now this first wind of the new year
whirls back out of the West
bringing the old months home.
What are we to do about time?
The blood and the havoc, the ceaseless machinations of power?
The griefs of the peoples?
Your passion pleases me. I fear the passion that kills.

Love, come flying on the wind
as when the beast's eyes first opened wide and he saw
in the brightest, bluest sky the depths
and the sweep of desire! He had no speech
to cry out, or even to whisper, "I am man!"
Has the human soul been born? We do have speech.

HOW MUCH EXPERIENCE DO WE NEED?

one slow full rich oblivion of loving
one sharp stab of death

        enough for a lifetime and a deathtime

        why so many
        seasons and days
        newspapers spilling over

when even
forsythia and daffodils
or one quick yellow-shafted flicker's return
can chill without warning?

3

LIKE
MORNING
LIGHT

SPARROW

A sparrow flew into
the cage of my mind
as I sat dreaming over
"Asphodel, That Greeny Flower"— how
surprised I was.

Into a globe filled with
light, rippling,
suddenly the cage was lowered,
in it a sparrow.

I looked again—true,
a sparrow!

    small, plump, slightly ruffled,
    there, perky, sitting, all of him

At one in the morning, half-sleeping, dreaming
over dear Williams's song of a dying old man's loves,
and grieving, privately, a heavy little grief all my own,
I found the rippling globe of light,
I found the lowered cage of my mind

    where a sparrow you could touch
    has come to stay.

GEOMETRIES OF HAIFA: NIGHT

The full moon explodes over the city—
and thrusts a glittering blade far over the sea.

    "We labor like pistons here."
    "It's dull."
    "Barbed wire encloses the full heart's garden here."

Arc of the moon and three stars over Haifa,
arc of the lights of Haifa below,
and the swordthrust of the full moon over the flat black sea.

LIKE MORNING LIGHT
*(An inscription for Eva E., 1918-1936, whom I knew as a child
in Passaic, N. J.)*

Russians, Poles, Jews— all die in this late November rain.
Outdoors, indoors, the same death-draught penetrates
whatever's only matter. Here in my head
the rain wanders, the clock unwinds, and the brave beam
of my desklamp grows duskily misty, revealing and hiding you.

Two children together, telling each other poems. If from your early
grave, you rose again now, onto the real streets, a real woman alive,
eyes still like myopic diamond knives vaguely piercing the mists,
a slight, sultry princess-slave slipping frailly amid the peasantry,
would I know the child I once saw in her bath and thought it music?
Yet you linger. Around you the stench of the Botany Mills and the
       stagnant Passaic.

You linger
gently, gaily, ignorant you are dying,
like the morning light over the Mount of Olives.

As all the bright children linger on the world's poisoned streets.

MY FRIEND'S ANGER

My friend is angry. He'd kill
those butcher-buffoons screwing all the nations—
betrayers of all the languages—
and even their bleating victims for being too damned dumb
to feel the shame when they get shafted.

His anger refuses to rest.
He quarrels with the very air for its indifference.
And with his own acquiescence— he earns a wage,
loves a girl, like every traitor
to honest poverty and the great human cause.

We want! to taste the snow, hear sweet words of pure thought, love
like angels who awoke this morning to find ourselves men.
"They" won't let us.
I too want to kill them
if their sodden lives could ever be restored.

We dwell within these tiny skulls.
We're primitives, we suck our charnel comforts.
The guts bulge through the transparency of our "minds."
Once and for all, to love the tentativeness of sweet thought
and to divide— share— our bread, love, souls, labors!

BITTER HONEY OF VIOLENCE

Rhetorician of your own agony, scooping
the pain of the world into the cornucopia of your particular pleasure
(emperor of that particular sort of ice-cream),

power cast loose from its moorings your great affect,

with one foot on the centrifugal and one on the centripetal horse,
domestically revolutionary, sentimentally toughminded, wise ass,
do you really think the cradle and the grave have the same address?

DEATHS OF THE POETS

Take the voices away
that pierce the always waiting ear,
splinters of God, biblical shell-fragments, screams
of police-sirens and out of the mouths
of dead faces holding steady in the mind's endless galleries—
voices that return and return and return.

Don't come too close.
I want to lift off.
I want to penetrate you. Don't you penetrate me.
I want to lift off from the red-hot ground
with my load of three-point-five billion passengers, my load
of three-point-five billion passengers screaming in here.

Touch a magnet, maybe I'll become one.
The ground's red-hot, and the sky,
and the air. They're jumping in front of the trucks
and from the bridges. They're shoving
their beautiful heads in the gas-ovens. They're
listening, listening, can't stop listening.

Touch a magnet, maybe I'll become one.
I want to lift off with my load—
three-point-five billion passengers treading down their dead,
stamping on baby faces, clawing each other down—
out to where there's no ground, no sky, no air,
no voice, not even silence, anywhere.

VISITING YEATS'S TOWER

Flourish or not, my vocation is to be
the poet of a lifetime, as was he,
and range that lifetime against my fantasy—
my poor knowledge against my threadbare belief.
I too must riddle, "Perfection of the life,
or of the work?"— must find my tower, bring my wife
and children up round the stairway, for all to see
them cower on the battlement with me.

A clown's hubris, to mask the naked face
with a still more naked, vulnerable grimace,
mimic the spiralings of our spinning race
with a sweaty bourgeois climb, and, at tower-top poised,
wheeze through a tickling throat: "Life? Work? My voice
cracks and wobbles, yet Song is my only choice!"
Resonant, impenetrable still, that place
we'd thought to reach, reality's sheer grace.

Reality is here, green, drowsy, around
Yeats's old pretentious tower, and the sound
of his leaping stream out-sings what my musings found.
Ballylee's here; and there, a mile off, lived
the Gregories. When troopers came by, Yeats grieved
that he could but dream what less brooding men achieved:
passionate action, that holds life and work spellbound—
real, murderous, even on this provincial ground.

MEMORY: A MEDITATION
AND A QUARREL WITH THE MASTER

"I died

before you could remember me again."

So a voice, in a dream itself hardly remembered. . . .

We can't get past Hamlet's questions, or even Hardy's.
Please forgive me. These heaps of human skulls (each
held eternity at bay, until eternity became
at one with mortality) do trouble my imagination sorely.
I quarrel with the master's beloved words. Man never "created death."

My argument a friend's battered Irish face, his smiling skull,
cracked on a stone when he dived in an unknown stream,
abandoning his hornrimmed battlements. Oh, well I know
his body was not bruised to pleasure Tom. There's no place
outside our skulls for that kind embittered face to live;
or that other's round, Roman face, great-eyed as Juno's. . . .

Merely friends' faces. Little history knows or cares.
I marshall these faces, call them back, bid them speak.
I alone remember them as I remember them.

I teach in the long classroom, questioning. The students,
burning or remote, reply or wait. Words that Tom and I, Henry and I,
held dear together, saying them with love, flow through the room
catching this soul or that into a kind of flame or light:
youthful recognition that pain and gaiety are one.
"The swan has leaped into the desolate heaven." Where's the old man
whose lunch I brought him daily when a child, our boarder shivering
in his small watchman's shack, the oily smoke
from his kerosene stove scalding my baby nostrils?
Where's my young stepfather I'd meet at the trolley station,
stumbling through snowstorms with his galoshes when he came home from
    work?
Where are the textile strikers lifting up their picket signs
through the long winter days of 1928? Where's their leader Weisbord?
    and the dream of the Union,
the songbursts of rage thrilling my childish heart?

                            Scattered
over wide America, the bones of men and women I loved

make one reply: *"We died*
before you could remember us again."

I've touched all I loved with the two poisoned blades:
the blade of my need, the blade of my fulfilment. While I stood
poised, the dancing died away. I turned my thoughts away
and all that awaited my return was gone. The cities forgot
my ghosts. The children of reality became the world, forgot
the blood-smeared streets of struggle while new demons
whipped them onward through other deaths.

                                        I stare at the sky
that glows as beautiful, as cold, as true to solitude
as when my mother walked upon the earth and dreamed
of how, when a girl, she'd dreamed
of returning home to Jónava to tell the peasants:
"Love one another, and the Jews, and lovely books and thoughts."